A New True Book

BASEBALL

By Ray Broekel

Children's Press®
A Division of Grolier Publishing
New York   London   Hong Kong   Sydney
Danbury, Connecticut

PHOTO CREDITS

AllSport — © Jonathan Daniel, 12 (left), 13; © Rick Stewart, 12 (right), 20 (left), 29 (right), 36; © Al Bello, 15 (left); © Andy Lyons, 20 (right); © Otto Greule, 27 (left), 29 (left), 33 (bottom), 34 (bottom); © Ken Levine, 27 (right); © Damian Strohmeyer, 31; © Stephen Dunn, 33 (top and center), 34 (top and center); © John Biever, 43

AP/ Wide World — 16

Unicorn Stock Photos — ©Aneal Vohra, cover, 25 (top right and bottom right); © Jeff Greenberg, 2; © Jim Shippee, 4, 7, 19, 23; © Eric R. Berndt, 8 (2 photos); © Kirk Schlea, 11; © Bill McMackins, 15 (right); © Mary Morina, 22; © J. L. Fly, 25 (left); © Martha McBride, 39; © Robert W. Ginn, 41 (left); © Steve Bourgeois, 41 (right)

UPI/Bettmann — 40

Cover — Kansas City Royals George Brett at bat

Library of Congress Cataloging-in-Publication Data

Broekel, Ray.
    Baseball / by Ray Broekel
        p. cm. — (A new true book)
    Includes index
    Summary: Describes briefly all aspects of baseball including the object of the game, the field, the equipment, positions, plays, teams, leagues, famous players, and games.
    ISBN 0-516-01081-6
    1. Baseball—Juvenile literature.
[1. Baseball.] I. Title.
GV867.5.B76   1995   95-17426
796.357'2—dc20   CIP AC

CONTENTS

BASEBALL IS FOR EVERYONE!

Baseball is played all over the world. The game was developed in the United States, but it is popular in Japan, Canada, Mexico, and many other Latin American countries.

Baseball is based on a game called rounders, which was played in England in the 1600s.

In 1845, Alexander J. Cartwright founded a baseball team in New York City. He wrote the first set of rules for the game.

In 1869, the Cincinnati Red Stockings became the first team to be paid to play ball. Later, other teams became professional.

There have been many changes in baseball since the 1890s, but the main parts of the game remain the same.

Kansas
City
Royals
Kauffman
Stadium

THE PLAYING FIELD

A baseball field is shaped like a diamond. At each corner of the diamond is a base. Each base is 90 feet from the next one. There is a first base, a second base, a third base, and homeplate.

7

Left: Grounds crew grooms home
plate and marks first base lines.
Right: A worker prepares the
pitcher's mound.

The playing field is
divided into three
sections: the infield, the
outfield, and foul territory.
In most parks, grass
covers the field. In some

parks, artificial turf covers the field.

The size and shape of an infield is always the same. But the size and shape of an outfield varies from one ballpark to another.

In the center of the infield is the pitcher's mound. It is 18 feet in diameter and rises gradually to 10 inches above the level of the field.

EQUIPMENT

    Major league baseball is played with a 9-to-9¼ inch ball that weighs between 5 and 5¼ ounces. The ball has a cork center, which is surrounded by layers of wool and cotton yarn. It is covered by cowhide sewn together with 108 stitches.

    Major league bats must be made of wood and can

A major league player might use as many as sixty bats a season. He hits a ball that is made of cork covered by 150 yards of cotton yarn, 219 yards of wool yarn, and cowhide.

be no more than 42 inches long and 2¾ inches in diameter. Other baseball leagues allow aluminum bats, which are lighter and almost never break.

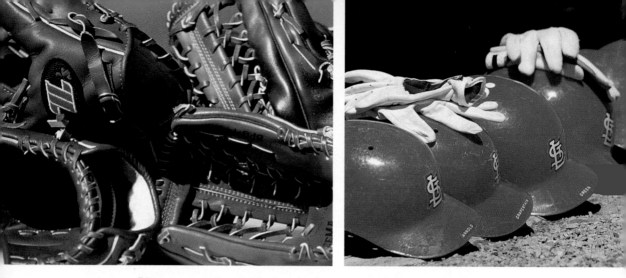

Players use three kinds of mitts — a catcher's mitt, first baseman's mitt, and a fielder's glove. They wear hard, plastic helmets when they are batting.

Each player uses a leather glove, or mitt. Mitts help players catch the ball. The padding on the mitts keeps players' hands from getting hurt.

Players wear a fabric baseball cap in the field.

When they bat, they put on a hard plastic batting helmet.

Catchers use special equipment for protection. They wear a helmet, a metal mask, a chest protector, and hard-plastic shin guards.

Catchers need protection from fast-pitched balls.

BATTERS AND BASE RUNNERS

A baseball game begins when a hitter, or batter, from the visiting team tries to hit a ball thrown by a pitcher from the home team.

Batters try to get on base. One way to get on base is to hit a ball and run to first base before a player from the opposite

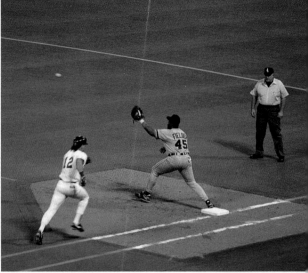

Left: San Diego Padres
Phil Plantier connects with
the ball. A good hitter
should also be a good
runner.

team throws the ball to
first base. This is called a
single.

When a hitter gets on
base, he or she is called a
"base runner." Then the
runner tries to move from

one base to another until he or she reaches home plate. Once the runner steps on home plate, a run is scored.

Sometimes a base runner will try to steal a base before a pitch is thrown. The runner has to slide into the base before an infielder gets the ball and tags him or her.

Toronto Blue Jays Devon White is safe at third after stealing a base.

If a runner gets to second base, it's called a double. If the runner goes to third base, it's a triple.

When a batter hits a ball over the outfield wall, it's a home run. A home run means that the player can advance around the bases without being tagged. He or she can step on home plate and score. If other runners are on base when a home run is hit, they will score, too.

PITCHERS AND CATCHERS

A pitcher's job is to get each hitter out. He or she stands on the pitching mound and throws the ball toward the batter. The batter can swing and try to hit the ball. Or, the batter can "take" the pitch, which means he lets it go by. If the batter takes the pitch

Fastballs thrown by some major league pitchers have been clocked at 100 miles per hour.

or swings and misses, the pitch is caught by the catcher.

The pitcher and his or her catcher decide how to throw the ball. A pitcher

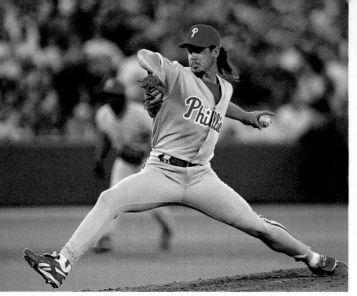

Left: Most pitchers are righthanded. Lefthanded pitchers are called "lefties," or "southpaws." Right: Los Angeles Dodgers catcher Mike Piazza, 1993 "Rookie of the Year"

can throw it high or low, inside or outside. He can also make it go fast or slow, straight or curved.

Pitchers throw fastballs, curveballs, knuckleballs, and sliders. They try to make hitters strike out.

THE STRIKE ZONE

A pitcher throws the ball through a 17-inch wide area above home plate. The area is the width of home plate and is called the "strike zone."

The strike zone goes from the batter's knees to his or her chest.

A batter can swing at any ball whether or not it

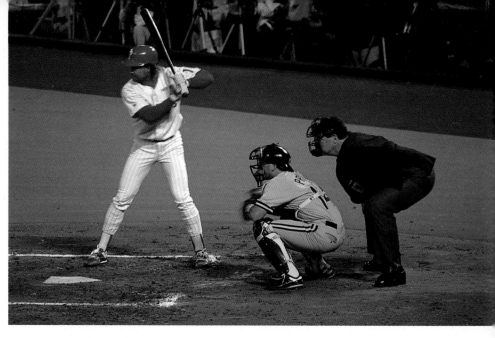

The batter and the umpire have only a split second to decide whether or not a pitch is good.

is in the strike zone. If he or she swings and misses the ball, the umpire calls a strike. If the pitch passes through any part of the strike zone, and the batter does not swing at it, it is also called a strike. Three strikes make an out.

Cleveland Indians batter checks his swing.

If a pitch misses the strike zone, and the batter does not swing at it, the umpire calls a "ball."

Four balls mean a walk. The batter goes to first base with a walk.

UMPIRES

Umpires judge a baseball game. Most major league games have four umpires.

Umpires stand near each of the four bases. The umpire behind the plate is in charge of the game. He decides when a pitch is good for hitting. He calls balls and strikes. He also gives the final ruling on all matters of the game.

Umpires' hand signals
indicate a strike (top left),
an out (top right), and
"safe" (bottom).

INFIELDERS

Infielders play near first, second, and third base. They try to catch a ball that is hit by an opposing player. It is their job to step on the base before a runner gets there. This "forces" the runner out. Infielders can also tag a base runner out before the runner reaches a base.

The infielder near third base is called the "third

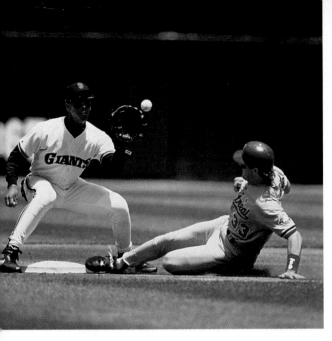

Infielders work together to get base runners out.

baseman." The second baseman plays near second base. The shortstop plays between second and third base. The first baseman plays near first base.

OUTFIELDERS

There are three outfielders. They try to catch balls that are hit to the outfield. When an outfielder catches a batted ball on the fly, the batter is out. When a batted ball drops in the outfield, the outfielder throws the ball to an infielder.

Outfielders New York Mets Barry
Bonds (left) and Toronto Blue Jays
Roberto Alomar (right)

The left fielder plays
between third and second
base. The center fielder
plays behind second base.
The right fielder plays
between second and first
base.

INNINGS

Most baseball games are nine innings long. Each team gets to bat in each inning. The visiting team bats first, or the "top" of the inning. The home team bats second, or the "bottom" of the inning. A team stays at bat until three outs are made.

The winning team is the one with the most runs

American League scoreboard worker takes a break.

after nine innings. If the
score is tied after nine
complete innings, the
game goes into extra
innings. The game ends
only when the score is not
tied after both teams have
batted in the extra inning.

THE MAJOR
LEAGUES

There are two major leagues — the American League and the National League. Fourteen teams play in each league. The leagues are split into three divisions each.

National League

Central Division
Cincinnati Reds
Chicago Cubs
Houston Astros
Pittsburgh Pirates
St. Louis Cardinals

Barry Larkin, Cincinnati Reds

East Division
Atlanta Braves
Florida Marlins
Montreal Expos
New York Mets
Philadelphia Phillies

Moises Alou, Montreal Expos

West Division
Colorado Rockies
Los Angeles Dodgers
San Diego Padres
San Francisco Giants

Hideo Nomo, Los Angeles Dodgers

American League

Central Division
Chicago White Sox
Cleveland Indians
Kansas City Royals
Milwaukee Brewers
Minnesota Twins

Frank Thomas,
Chicago White Sox

East Division
Baltimore Orioles
Boston Red Sox
Detroit Tigers
New York Yankees
Toronto Blue Jays

Roberto Alomar,
Toronto Blue Jays

West Division
California Angels
Oakland Athletics
Seattle Mariners
Texas Rangers

Ken Griffey Jr.,
Seattle Mariners

THE WORLD SERIES

Following a season of
162 games, each league's
three division winners plus
one "wildcard" team play
in the playoffs. They play
for the league title, or
"pennant." The American
and National League
champions then compete
in the World Series.

Joe Carter's 9th inning homerun for the Toronto Blue Jays
clinched the 1993 World Series.

In the World Series, a team must win four out of seven games. Then it becomes that year's champion of baseball.

Major college teams compete in the College World Series. This tournament is held every year in Omaha, Nebraska.

LITTLE LEAGUE AND T-BALL

Today there are baseball leagues for every level of play. For boys and girls between the ages of eight and twelve, there's Little League. For 13-to-15 year-olds, there's the Senior League. And there's the Big League for 16-to-18 year-olds.

Girls softball tournament

The Senior Leagues and
Big Leagues play on a
regular-size diamond with
rules similar to those in the
major leagues.

The Little League, however, has different rules. The distance between bases is only 60 feet, and the pitching and outfield distances are shorter, too.

The Little League World Series is held every year and invites teams from around the world.

Little League World Series game between Europe and the Far East

Hopeful T-Ball players

Boys and girls who want
to play baseball, but are
not yet eight years old, can
play T-Ball. Everyone can
have fun playing a game
that is one of America's
favorite sports.

Famous Professional Players

Hank Aaron, Atlanta Braves, Milwaukee Brewers

Roger Clemens, Boston Red Sox

Ty Cobb, Detroit Tigers, Philadelphia Athletics

Joe DiMaggio, New York Yankees

Lou Gehrig, New York Yankees

Ken Griffey, Jr., Seattle Mariners

Roger Hornsby, St. Louis Cardinals, New York Giants, Boston Braves, Chicago Cubs, St. Louis Browns

Reggie Jackson, Kansas City/Oakland Athletics, Baltimore Orioles, New York Yankees, California Angels

Sandy Koufax, Los Angeles Dodgers

Greg Maddox, Chicago Cubs, Atlanta Braves

Mickey Mantle, New York Yankees

Willie Mays, New York/San Francisco Giants, New York Mets

Stan Musial, St. Louis Cardinals

Cal Ripken, Jr., Baltimore Orioles

Jackie Robinson, Brooklyn Dodgers

Pete Rose, Cincinnati Reds, Philadelphia Phillies, Montreal Expos, Boston Red Sox

Babe Ruth, New York Yankees, Boston Braves

Nolan Ryan, New York Mets, California Angels, Houston Astros, Texas Rangers

Ted Williams, Boston Red Sox

Cy Young, Cleveland Spiders, St. Louis Cardinals, Boston Red Sox, Cleveland Indians, Boston Braves

Nolan Ryan, Texas Rangers

GLOSSARY

aluminum (ă loo´mă nŭm) — a
   lightweight silver metal

artificial (ar te fĭsh´el) — not natural;
   made by people

ball — a pitch that is not good; a pitch
   that is not thrown into the strike zone

base runner (bās run´er) — in baseball,
   a person who runs to a base after
   hitting a ball

champion (chăm´pē en) — the winner; the
   best

diamond (dī´a mend) — that part of a
   baseball field that makes up the infield

fabric (făb´rĭk) — cloth

foul ball — a batted ball that lands
   outside the foul lines

infield (ĭn´ fēld) — the part of a baseball field that is inside the bases

inning (ĭn´ĭng)— the part of a baseball game in which each team comes to bat

league (lēg) — a group of sports teams

mound — small hill on which a baseball pitcher stands

outfield (out´ fēld) — that part of a baseball field beyond the bases

pennant (pĕn´ent) — a flag that means a team is the champion of a league

pitch (pĭch) — to throw or toss

shin (shĭn) — the front part of the leg between the knee and the ankle

strike (strīk) — a pitched ball, which crosses home plate within the strike zone, that a batter swings at but misses

strike out — to get a batter out with three strikes

turf — the top layer of grassy land; sod

umpire (ŭm´pīre) — a person who rules on plays

INDEX

ABOUT THE AUTHOR

Ray Broekel is a full-time freelance writer who lives with his wife, Peg, and a dog, Fergus, in Ipswich, Massachusetts. He has had twenty years of experience as a children's book editor and newspaper supervisor, and has taught many subjects in kindergarten through college levels.

Dr. Broekel has had over 1,000 stories and articles published, and over 100 books. His first book was published in 1956 by Children's Press.

Accelerated Reader